AF488402

Written and Illustrated by ©Mariia Furdei
First Edition, 2022

Follow
Instagram: @MariiaFurdei
Web: www.mariafurdei.com

Acknowledgments

I want to thank my dear family and friends.
Your incredible support and endless patience made this possible.

All proceeds from this book will be donated to non-profit organizations and funds that are assisting children affected by the war in Ukraine.

For more information please visit https://www.mariafurdei.com/lightofhope

LIGHT
OF HOPE
by Mariia Furdei

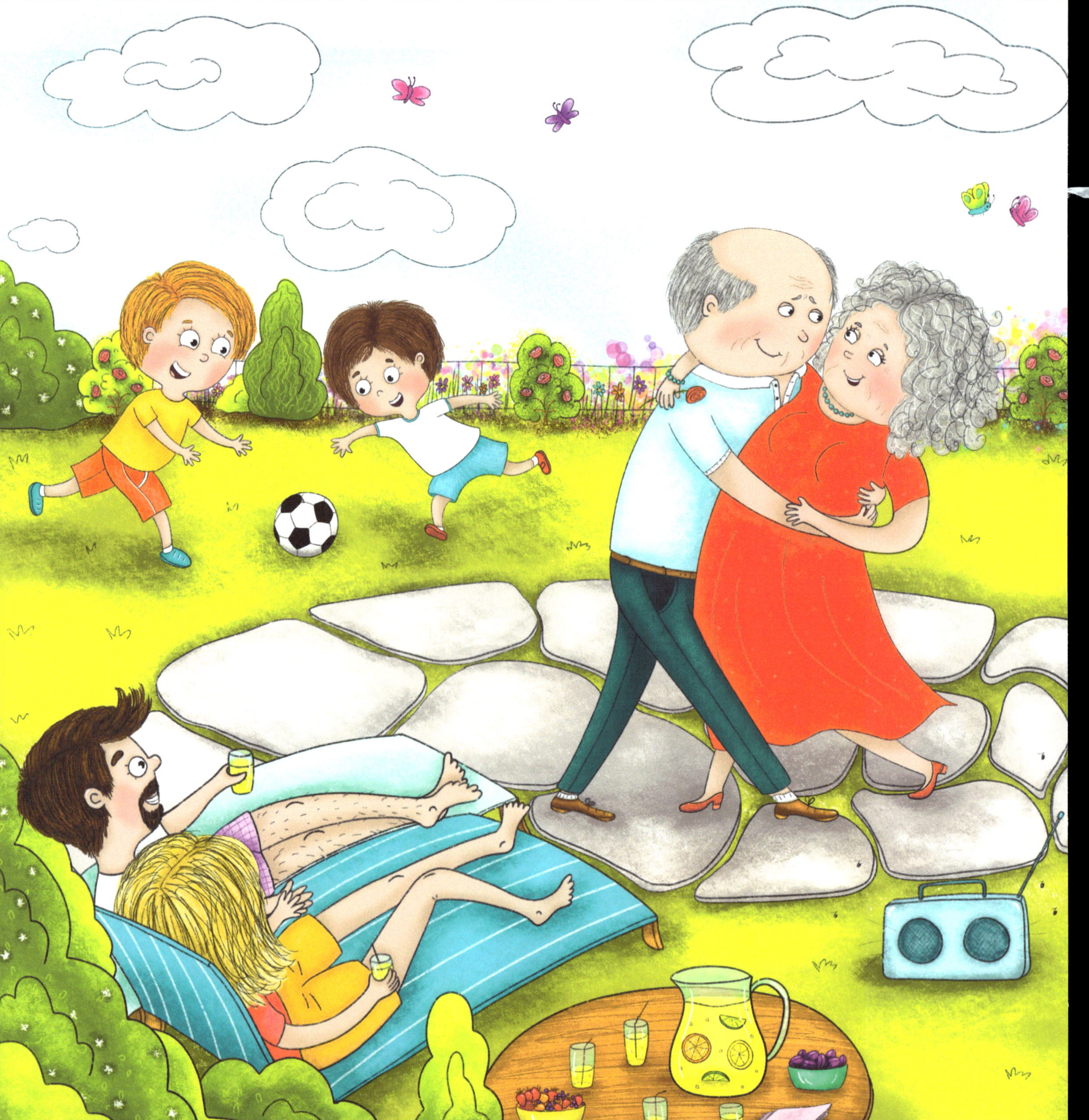

It was a nice and happy day.

My grandparents danced to their favorite music.

And I played with my friends.

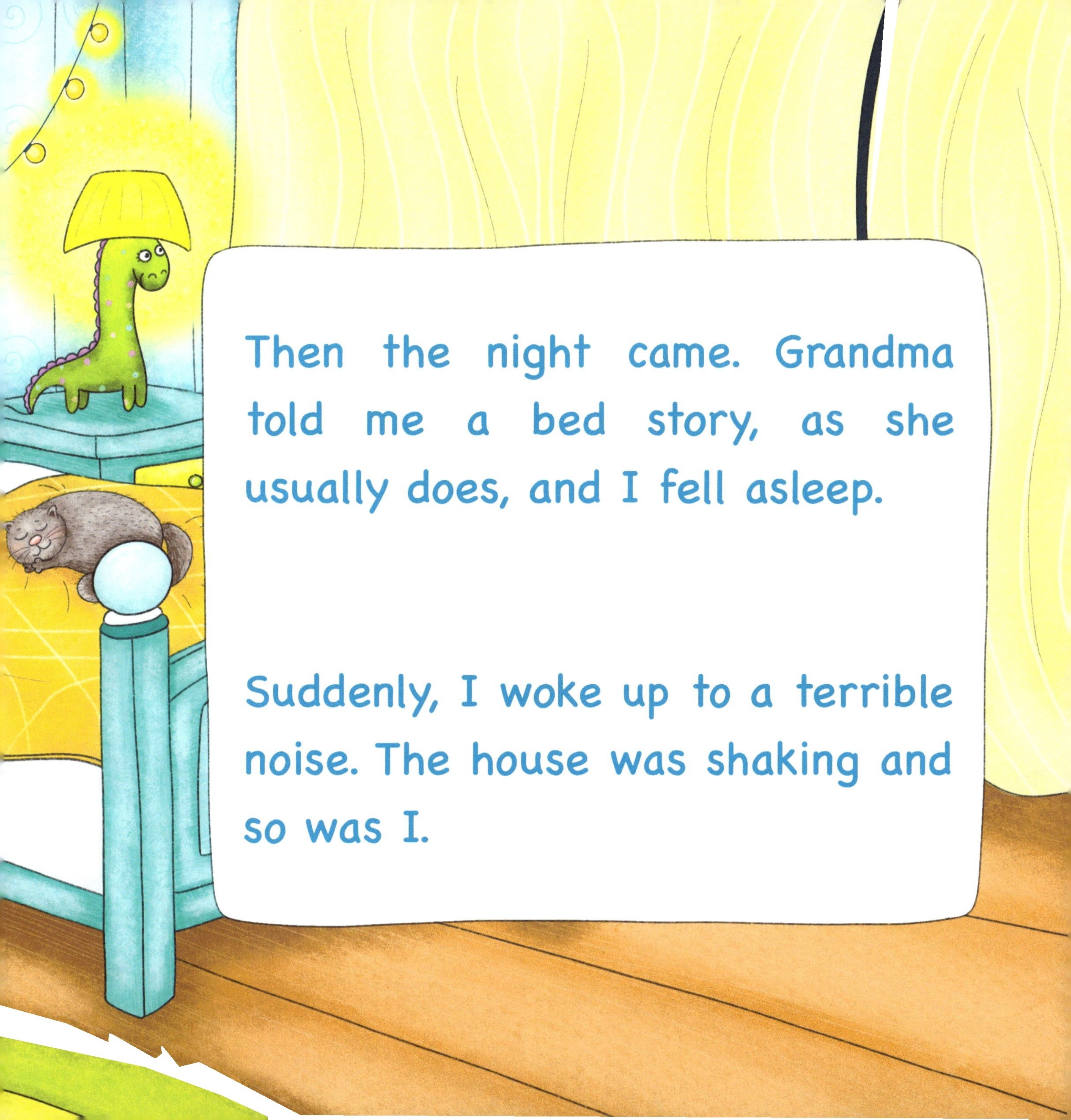

Then the night came. Grandma told me a bed story, as she usually does, and I fell asleep.

Suddenly, I woke up to a terrible noise. The house was shaking and so was I.

It was dark

and loud,

and so very scary.

My mom told me to put my boots and jacket on.

She packed some things into her bag and we left to go somewhere in a big hurry.

Now my family and I have to hide in the dark.

My mom says this place is called a bomb shelter.

We can't go outside.

We hear explosions day and night.

I get scared when
bombs rumble,
walls shake,
and explosions light up the sky.

But when we hold each other's hands and talk, I get a little less scared.

Mom explains this is war, but she will keep me safe. Yet when she hugs me tight, I feel her tremble and cry.

I often feel sad and helpless.

I have photos of my loved ones.

Looking at them makes me feel better.

When I cuddle with Grandma and Mom, I forget about the war.

It gives me a light of hope.

And a hope we could all live in peace.

Mariia Furdei

About the author

Mariia Furdei is a Ukrainian illustrator based in California USA. She has a lifelong love for drawing and art since she found her mom's lipstick and made her first drawing on the wall.

She managed to help her parents, who were able to leave Kiev after living in a cellar without heat for days. Her brother, other relatives and friends are still in Ukraine.

Mariia wants to increase people's awareness about the war in Ukraine and to help children that were affected by the war in Ukraine.

All proceeds from this book will be donated
to non-profit organizations and funds that
are assisting children affected by the war
in Ukraine.

For more information please visit https://www.mariafurdei.com/lightofhope

* 9 7 9 8 9 8 7 6 8 3 0 0 2 *